World Traveler

Travel to Italy

Matt Doeden

Lerner Publications ◆ Minneapolis

Content consultant: Lorenzo Fabbri, University of Minnesota

Lerner Publications Company
An imprint of Lerner Publishing Group, Inc.
241 First Avenue North
Minneapolis, MN 55401 USA

For reading levels and more information, look up this title
at www.lernerbooks.com.

Main body text set in Adrianna Regular.
Typeface provided by Chank.

Map illustration on page 29 by Laura K. Westlund.

Library of Congress Cataloging-in-Publication Data

Names: Doeden, Matt, author.
Title: Travel to Italy / Matt Doeden.
Description: Minneapolis : Lerner Publications, [2023] | Series: Searchlight books - world traveler | Includes bibliographical references and index. | Audience: Ages 8–11 | Audience: Grades 4–6 | Summary: "Stretching into the Mediterranean Sea, Italy is known for its cuisine, cities, and cultures. Learn about Italy's history from the Roman Empire to the present and uncover its geography and landscapes"— Provided by publisher.
Identifiers: LCCN 2022016315 (print) | LCCN 2022016316 (ebook) | ISBN 9781728457888 (lib. bdg.) | ISBN 9781728463971 (pbk.) | ISBN 9781728461953 (eb pdf)
Subjects: LCSH: Italy—Juvenile literature.
Classification: LCC DG417 .D64 2023 (print) | LCC DG417 (ebook) | DDC 945—dc23/eng/20220415

LC record available at https://lccn.loc.gov/2022016315
LC ebook record available at https://lccn.loc.gov/2022016316

Manufactured in the United States of America
1-50816-50155-8/1/2022

Table of Contents

Chapter 1

GEOGRAPHY AND CLIMATE

From the towering peaks of the Alps to rolling hills and long coastlines, Italy is filled with beauty and a rich history.

Italy is in western Europe. Most of the country forms a boot-shaped peninsula that stretches into the Mediterranean Sea toward the African coastline. Italy also includes the islands of Sardinia and Sicily. It covers 116,348 square miles (301,340 sq. km).

The Land

The Mediterranean Sea surrounds most of Italy's western, southern, and eastern borders. Northern Italy borders Slovenia, Austria, Switzerland, and France. The independent city-state of Vatican City lies within Italy.

Italy has an alpine region in the north. Mountains dominate the landscape. The Alps lie where Italy borders Switzerland and France. Monte Bianco (White Mountain) of Courmayeur is there. Its peak stands 15,577 feet (4,748 m) above sea level.

Italy has open plains and long coastlines. The Po Valley is a large, flat lowland. Its fertile soils grow much of Italy's crops. The Apulian Plain in the south is a rugged land.

Rivers and Lakes

The Po is the longest river in Italy. It flows 405 miles (652 km) from the Alps to the Adriatic Sea. The Po flows through several major cities. Pollution of its waters from farmland runoff is a major problem. The Tiber River runs through the center of the country and passes through Rome.

One of the cities that the Po River flows through is Turin, Italy.

LAKE GARDA HAS 77.5 MILES (125 KM) OF SHORELINE.

Lake Garda is Italy's largest lake. This popular vacation spot lies in northern Italy, along the edge of the Dolomite mountain range. The lake covers about 143 square miles (370 sq. km). Lake Maggiore and Lake Como are other popular recreational lakes in Italy.

Must-See Stop:
The Canals of Venice

Venice is a city with no cars. Canals and bridges connect the city. Venice is in a lagoon, or enclosed bay, in northern Italy. The city on water includes more than one hundred islands. People cross the city on boats called gondolas.

Climate

Italy has a varied climate. South and central Italy have hot, dry summers and cool, wet winters. The country is warmest in the south and coldest in the north.

In northern Italy, temperatures generally drop with elevation. Snowfall and rain are abundant throughout much of this region. Many of the country's mountain ranges are covered in snow from November to May.

Chapter 2

HISTORY AND GOVERNMENT

Humans have lived in Italy since prehistorical times. Archaeologists don't know exactly when humans first appeared in what is now Europe. It was probably between thirty-five thousand and fifty-five thousand years ago.

Many cultures emerged in Italy. The Etruscan people created a vibrant community. From about 700 BCE to 200 BCE, they lived across much of present-day Italy. They were skilled builders and traded with other Mediterranean cultures.

The Roman Era

Italy's past helps shape its present. Its capital, Rome, was built around 750 BCE along the Tiber River.

In 509 BCE, Rome became a republic. Its leaders met in counsels and in the Senate to rule Rome and pass laws. The Romans fought wars to expand their territory. Rome included parts of modern Europe, Africa, and Asia. They controlled neighboring lands and the people who lived there. But many people did not want to live under Roman rule. They wanted to be independent, so they rose up against their invaders.

The Temple of Saturn was built sometime between 501 BCE and 497 BCE in Rome.

Rome faced constant rebellions. General Julius Caesar took over Rome by centralizing power. He turned Rome from a republic into an empire. He ruled until his death.

The Roman Empire remained powerful for hundreds of years. But by the 400s CE, Rome was falling apart. People continued to rebel against the empire, and it collapsed in 476 CE. The people who they invaded were free from Rome's colonization. Rome became a city again. Italy split into many smaller states.

Must-See Stop:
The Colosseum

The Colosseum is in Rome, a city known for its ancient ruins. Few sites compare to the amphitheater built two thousand years ago. In ancient Rome, the Colosseum held gladiator fights and other exciting events. Millions of visitors tour the site each year. They marvel at the ancient architecture and its history.

A New Era

In the 1500s, the Renaissance movement started in Italy. It sparked people's interest in science and art. Many people think of the Renaissance as marking the time between the ancient world and the modern world.

But trouble followed. Several plagues spread across Italy. War and power struggles led to unstable leadership. In 1796, French military leader Napoleon Bonaparte conquered much of Italy.

Starting in 1815, Italian states slowly started to unite. In 1861, states joined to form a new nation, Italy.

War and Rebirth

Italy fought in World War I (1914–1918) alongside Germany
and Austria. They lost the war. World War I veteran
Benito Mussolini rose to power in 1922. Later, he became
a dictator and had complete control of the country.

Mussolini formed an alliance with German leader Adolf
Hitler. Hitler, the head of Germany's Nazi Party, wanted
to expand Germany's territory and suppress people from

Mussolini was
a dictator who
controlled
Italy from
1922 to 1943.

certain ethnic, religious, and sexual groups. In World War II (1939–1945), Italy fought alongside Nazi Germany. The long, bloody war was hard on Italy and its people. In the final days of the war in Europe, Mussolini was captured and killed. Italy surrendered to the Allies, but it was still controlled by Nazi Germany. Later, the United States helped defeat the Nazis in Italy.

Germany and Italy lost the war. Italy's economy was crushed. The country rebuilt as a republic. By the 1950s, the economy had recovered. Over the following decades, the country still suffered from political instability. But conditions were improving for its people.

Government

Italy's government is a democratic republic. People vote for their leaders. The president is the head of state. The three branches of government are legislative, executive, and judicial.

The legislative branch makes laws. It has two chambers, the Senate and the Chamber of Deputies. The executive branch enforces laws. The prime minister is the head of this branch. The judicial branch applies the law. The Constitutional Court rules on whether laws follow the constitution.

Sergio Mattarella was elected to a second term as Italy's president in 2022.

Chapter 3

CULTURE AND PEOPLE

With more than sixty-one million people, Italy is the world's twenty-third most populous country. Italians share a culture that is rich in art, music, food, and more. Many Italians have ancestry beyond Italy. Their families come from many places including Germany, France, Slovenia, Romania, Albania, Morocco, Iraq, Afghanistan, Bangladesh, Egypt, El Salvador, Peru, China, the Philippines, Pakistan, and India. Romani people in Italy were originally nomads but then put

down roots in cities such as Milan, Turin, and Rome. They enrich these places with their oral traditions and folk music.

Religion

About 81 percent of Italians are Christians. Vatican City is the home of the Roman Catholic faith. Most Christian Italians are Roman Catholics. The Catholic Church started there when Rome adopted Christianity as its official religion in 323 CE.

About 5 percent of Italians are Muslims. They follow the Islamic faith. Islam came to Italy in the 800s CE.

Less than 1 percent of Italians belong to other religions, such as Judaism or Hinduism. And 13 percent of Italians do not follow any religion.

Vatican City covers 0.17 square miles (0.44 sq. km).

Language and Writing

Italy's official language is Italian. Other languages spoken in Italy include German, French, Greek, Albanian, Ladin, Slovene, Sardu, Friulian, and Occitan.

Italian evolved from a type of Latin that was spoken in ancient Italy. In modern times, several dialects of Italian exist. People have little trouble understanding speakers of another dialect.

Similar to English, Italian uses the Roman alphabet. But the Italian alphabet uses only twenty-one characters. The letters *j, k, w, x,* and *y* are not used in Italian words. They are only used in words that come from other languages.

Students practice their writing in Milan, Italy.

Food and Art

Italy is famous for its cuisine. Italian dishes often use basil, thyme, oregano, rosemary, garlic, and onions as well as other herbs and spices. Many meals are built around pasta covered in rich sauces. Fish, seafood, and other meats often follow. And of course, Italy is the birthplace of pizza.

Art is central to Italy's culture. It is the home of legendary artists such as Michelangelo, Raphael, Leonardo da Vinci, and Caravaggio. Classic Italian architecture often includes bold geometric forms, arches, and columns.

Let's Celebrate:
Liberation Day

Italy fought with the Axis powers during World War II. But many of its people stood against that alliance. Each year on April 25 they celebrate Liberation Day. It celebrates the day when Italian resistance overthrew Nazi rule in Italy. People gather in town squares to attend

parades, concerts, and political rallies. Airplanes paint the sky with the colors of Italy's flag. Many people place wreaths on war monuments to honor the people who died in the struggle.

Chapter 4

DAILY LIFE

Most Italians live in urban areas. Rome is the nation's capital and largest city, with about 4.3 million people. Other major cities include Milan (3.1 million), Naples (2.2 million), and Turin (1.8 million).

The fashion industry, tourism, and food service are some of Italy's biggest employers. About 68 percent of Italians work in the service industry. About 24 percent work in manufacturing. They produce goods such as

metals, machinery, and clothing. About 4 percent of Italians work in agriculture. They grow crops such as grapes, wheat, corn, tomatoes, olives, and apples. A lot of foreign workers and migrants work in Italian fields as well, contributing to nurturing the nation.

Italian children from six through sixteen must attend school. Children go to school six days a week—including Saturdays. With five hours of class each day, their school days are shorter than those of US schools. About one-third of adults have a high school diploma. This number is rising among younger generations.

Let's Celebrate:
Battle of the Oranges

Would you like to be part of the biggest food fight in Italy? Head to the town of Ivrea in February for a party unlike any other. Nine teams hurl oranges at one another in the town square while a panel of judges looks on and chooses a winner. By the time the fighting is over, the ground is covered in orange peels and pulp. Anyone can take part, but most are happy just to watch.

Looking to the Future

A large wealth gap poses a future challenge for Italy. A small number of people have most of the country's wealth. About 10 percent of the population lives below the poverty line. Italy has taken steps to decrease poverty rates. Many Italians are optimistic that poverty will continue to decline.

About 8 percent of Italians are unemployed. The majority are young people, women, and people of color, who face barriers to finding good-paying jobs.

Climate change is another concern for Italy. As temperatures rise, so do sea levels. Seaside towns and cities could go underwater. Changes in rainfall patterns and temperature could threaten agriculture. Italy is taking steps to prepare for these changes and to slow future changes. It's protecting and growing its forest lands. It's lowering its fossil fuel use. Italians understand the dangers of climate change. They're hopeful that they can be part of a global effort to control the problem and build a brighter future for their country.

Map and Key Facts

Flag of Italy

- Continent: Europe
- Capital city: Rome
- Population: sixty-one million
- Languages: about thirty-four languages including Italian, German, Spanish, Basque, Arabic, French, and Slovenian

Glossary

architecture: the style and form of buildings

dictator: a leader who has total power over a country

elevation: height above sea level

empire: a collection of states under the rule of a single authority, often called an emperor

peninsula: a piece of land that juts out into a body of water

plague: an outbreak of a widespread and deadly disease

poverty: the condition of being poor

Renaissance: a movement in the fifteenth and sixteenth centuries that focused on art, science, learning, and exploration

republic: a state in which power is held by elected representatives

Learn More

Ainsley, Dominic J. *Italy.* Broomall, PA: Mason Crest, 2019.

Bell, Samantha. *Ancient Rome.* Lake Elmo, MN: Focus Readers, 2020.

Britannica Kids: Italy
    https://kids.britannica.com/students/article/Italy/275105

Kids World Travel Guide: Italy
    https://www.kids-world-travel-guide.com/italy-facts.html

Layton, Christine. *Travel to Germany.* Minneapolis: Lerner Publications, 2023.

National Geographic Kids: Italy
    https://kids.nationalgeographic.com/geography/countries/article/italy

Index

Photo Acknowledgments

Image credits: macumazahn/Shutterstock, p. 5; AleksandarGeorgiev/Getty Images, p. 6; Lukasz Szwaj/Shutterstock, p. 7; Seng Chye Teo/Getty Images, p. 8; Mau47/Shutterstock, p. 9; Julian Elliott Photography/Getty Images, p. 11; lynea/Shutterstock, p. 12; Hippo1947/ Shutterstock, p. 13; Wynnter/Getty Images, p. 14; Photos.com/Getty Images, p. 15; Keystone/ Hulton Archive/Stringer/Getty Images, p. 16; Antonio Masiello/Getty Images, p. 17; as-artmedia/ Shutterstock, p. 19; iamcu4tro/Shutterstock, p. 20; MikeDotta/Shutterstock, p. 21; ArxOnt/ Getty Images, p. 22; Roberto Serra - Iguana Press/Getty Images, p. 23; Olgaviare/Getty Images, p. 25; Rita Bredeson/Shutterstock, p. 26; pawel.gaul/Getty Images, p. 27; © Marco Bottigelli/Getty Images, p. 28; Laura Westlund, p. 29.

Cover: Sol de Zuasnabar Brebbia/Getty Images.